MAKING ART WITH PACKAGING

Gillian Chapman & Pam Robson

PowerKiDS press.

New York

All projects should be done carefully, with an adult's help and supervision wh

appropriate (especially for activities involving any cutting, carving, or sewing). A

adult should execute or supervise any work with a craft knife, and safety scisso

should be used for all cutting.

Published in 2008 by The Rosen Publishing Group, Inc.
29 East 21st Street, New York, NY 10010

Copyright © 2008 Wayland/The Rosen Publishing Group, Inc.

First Edition

Picture Acknowledgments
Ecoscene 4b (Sally Morgan), 5t (Whatmore),
Lois Walpole 4t, 5b

Library of Congress Cataloging-in-Publication Data

Chapman, Gillian.
Making Art with packaging / Gillian Chapman & Pam Robson. -- 1st e⋅
    p. cm. -- (Everyday art)
    Includes index.
     ISBN-13: 978-1-4042-3724-7 (library binding)
    ISBN-10: 1-4042-3724-0 (library binding)
   1. Packaging--Juvenile literature. 2. Recycling (Waste, etc.)
 Juvenile literature. 3. Paper work--Juvenile literature. 4. Plastic
    craft--Juvenile literature. 5. Aluminum foil craft--Juvenile
    literature. I. Robson, Pam. II. Title.
 TT160.C49 2007
 745.5--dc22
                                    2006028319

Manufactured in China

Contents

What Is Packaging?

The Importance of Packaging

In the United States and Europe during the nineteenth century, people did their shopping at a general store. Dry goods, such as cereals, sugar, and tea, were individually weighed then packed in twists of paper and wrappings of the shopkeeper's own design.

The first mass-produced paper bags were made in Pennsylvania in 1852, but it was the production of the folding carton that revolutionized packaging. Cartons could be used to package a wide variety of products. Packaging soon became as important as the product itself.

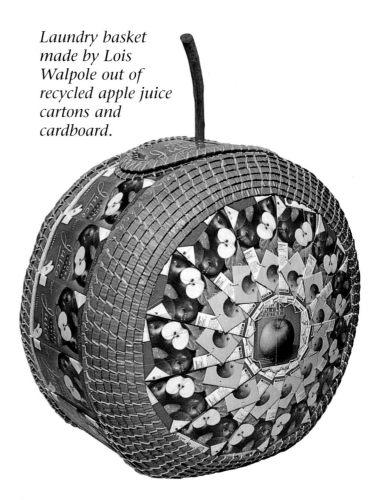

Laundry basket made by Lois Walpole out of recycled apple juice cartons and cardboard.

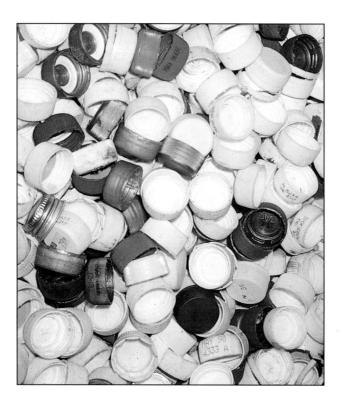

Plastic bottle tops can be used in a variety of art projects.

The Purpose of Packaging

Packaging is a term used to describe a vast range of materials and containers. Its purpose is to protect and advertise the products we purchase in our stores. Packaging becomes worthless and disposable once its contents are used. Cardboard boxes, tubes, cans, plastic tapes and wires, cartons, bottle tops, and labels are some of the items you can collect. They do have value and this book makes some exciting suggestions for putting to good use packaging that might once have been considered garbage.

Precycling

About 30 percent of manufactured plastic is used for packaging; about half the weight of the plastic we throw away is packaging. One way to help avoid this waste is to *precycle*, which means to stop buying goods packaged in layers of unnecessary plastic wrappers. Buy drinks in glass bottles and aluminum cans that can be recycled.

Aluminum cans reused as building material in Botswana, Africa.

Recycling Packaging

Aluminum cans are about 20 percent cheaper to recycle than to make and need 5 percent of the energy. In Padua, Italy, a model of the Basilica Sant'Antonio has been erected using 3,250,000 cans, collected from streets and homes. In 1992, Sweden collected 787 million cans. How many can you collect and recycle?

During the Second World War (1939–1945), people were asked to salvage all useful items that might otherwise have been discarded. Trash was sorted into separate bins. Present day recycling points are organized in the same way. Scrap iron was claimed by the government for munitions, even iron railings were removed, and aluminum saucepans were turned into airplanes. Modern packagers can reuse aluminum, glass, paper, and cardboard — make sure you sort your trash and take it to your local collection point.

A large dish made by Lois Walpole from used cans.

Printing Patterns

Printing Blocks

Printing blocks are traditionally made from wood; the harder the wood, the more delicate the carving. These blocks interlock so that a repeating pattern can be accurately printed over a large area. Indian craftworkers are highly skilled at producing intricate designs printed on cotton textiles.

You can use a wide variety of packaging materials to make exciting patterns. Simple printing blocks can be made from polystyrene packing (styrofoam). The blocks are easy to carve and shape, yet are firm enough to use many times.

Prints made with packaging

Textured Prints

To make a textured print, find a large piece of textured wrapping, such as bubblewrap or corrugated cardboard. Cover this with colored ink, or paint and press gently on a piece of plain paper. Leave it to dry, then carefully peel off the wrapping. It will have left a colorful, textured pattern.

This kind of print is called a *monoprint.* The wrapping cannot be used again in the same way, which makes every print unique. With repeated printing methods, each print made from the same block is identical, and prints can be made until the block wears out.

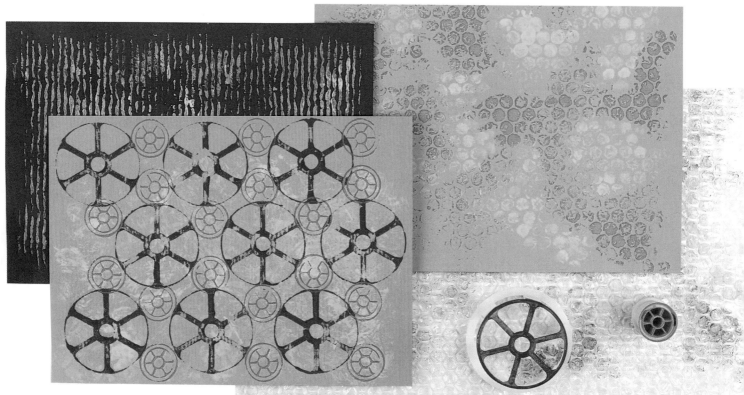

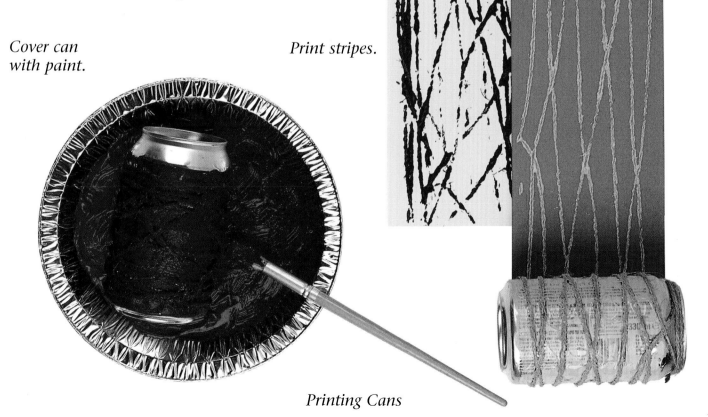

Wind string around a can to make a pattern.

Repeating Patterns

Many items of packaging make ideal printing tools. Plastic spools and lids come in a variety of interesting shapes and sizes. See what you can find and experiment with different types. Use them to print repeating patterns and designs on the textured prints.

Printing Cans

Another way of making a repeating print involves using an empty drink can. Wind pieces of string around the can to make a pattern, and tie the string firmly in place. Cover the can in paint, so that the string picks up all the color. Then slowly roll it over a strip of paper. You can see the results in the examples shown here.

Cover can with paint.

Print stripes.

Printing Cans

Packaging Prints

Printed Gift wrap

It is now common for gift wrap and greeting cards to be printed on recycled paper. By printing your own paper, you are being environmentally aware and avoiding further waste. You can produce unusual designs for special occasions.

Printed Pictures

A portfolio is a useful storage container for your prints. They can also be displayed in frames made from recycled materials. In this way you create a complete "salvaged" work of art.

Finished Portfolio

Place strong tape diagonally across the corners of the portfolio covers.

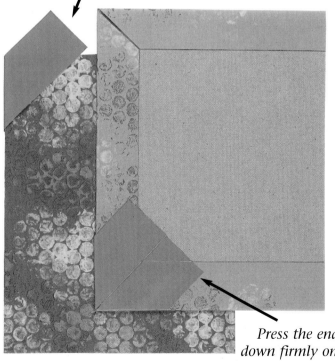

Press the ends down firmly on the back of the cardboard.

Taping the Corners of the Portfolio

Making a Portfolio

The size of the portfolio you make will depend upon the size of your artwork. The measurements given here are for a portfolio designed to store large prints.

Cut two large pieces of scrap cardboard 25 in (65 cm) by 17½ in (45 cm). Cover the outside of the cardboard using your own printed paper, taping across the corners for extra protection. Cover the inside of both pieces of cardboard, again using printed paper.

Tape the covers together along the longest sides. Make flaps to fit inside one of the covers, and glue them in place to hold the artwork. Cut slots in the two covers, and thread tape through to fasten the portfolio.

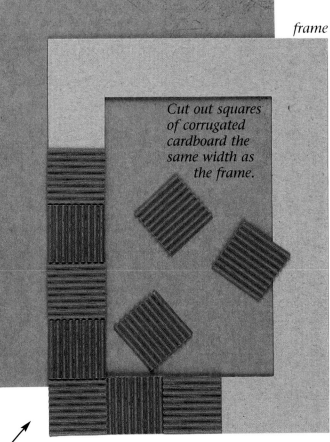

Cut out squares of corrugated cardboard the same width as the frame.

Picture Frames

To make a frame to fit a particular piece of artwork, you will need to work to precise measurements. Cut a frame from stiff cardboard, making the window opening 1¾ in (2 cm) smaller than the print. The width of the frame should be 2½ in (6 cm) around. Make backing cardboard the same size as the frame.

The frames shown here have been covered with squares of corrugated cardboard, crumpled foil, and colored twine. Decorate the frame and paint it first before attaching the backing cardboard. Finally, mount your print between them. Glue a strip of cardboard to the back of the frame to give it support.

Build up a pattern along the frame.

Making Picture Frames

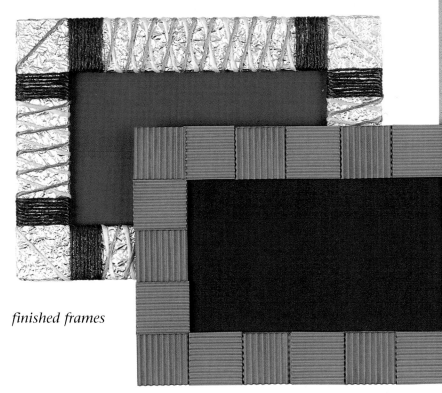

finished frames

back view

9

Plastic Art

Plastics

Some plastics are biodegradable, most are not. It is possible to melt down certain plastic items for reuse in another form. The rest must be burned, causing toxic fumes, or dumped into landfall sites, creating methane gas, which can be dangerous. Soft-drink bottles made from polyethylene terephthalate (PET) can be melted down and turned into a cottonlike fiber. This can be used as insulation or even for new carpets.

Plastic Products

Look around you and see how much plastic has been used and discarded. Start to make a plastic collection that can be used for project work. Plastic bags and wrappings, tapes and twines are perfect for craftwork — the more colorful they are, the better.

Woven Placemats

Colorful placemats can be made from different types of plastic tapes and twine woven and twisted around cardboard shapes. Cut out the placemat shape from a piece of scrap cardboard, and make notches along the two opposite sides. Wind thin, flexible plastic twine or wire around the notches, as shown here. Then weave across the twine with thicker tape. The finished placemats are both attractive and practical.

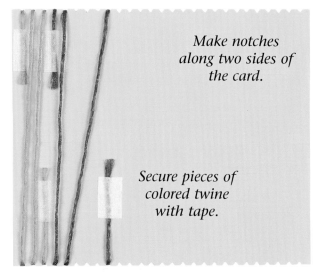

Make notches along two sides of the card.

Secure pieces of colored twine with tape.

making the frame

finished placemat

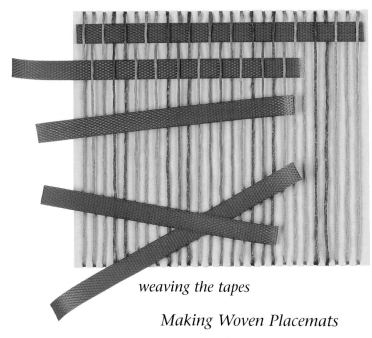

weaving the tapes

Making Woven Placemats

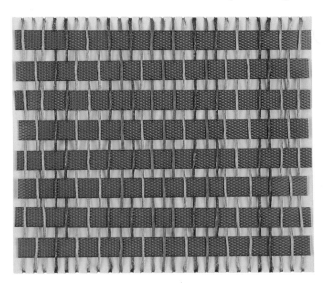

Plastic Twine and Packaging

Purposeful Projects

In the 1950s, the mass-production of flexible plastic made it ideal for packaging. It was clean, cheap, and malleable. Until recently, manufacturers used it without any thought for the environmental consequences.

By using nonrecyclable packaging for purposeful projects, you can make a positive contribution toward reducing the size of the garbage mountains, and help conserve Earth's natural resources.

Plastic Picture

Plastic Pictures

Weaving a picture out of plastic materials makes use of a wide range of disposable packaging. First, you will need to draw a simple picture on paper, then place a piece of plastic net over the top. Weave different colored pieces of plastic in and out of the net following the design behind the mesh. Choose colors and textures that fit the subject. Mount the finished picture on a plastic backing.

Woven Baskets

Natural Baskets

Palm fronds were the first fans. Whole leaves were the first umbrellas. The first baskets were woven using common natural materials, usually rattans. Baskets can be made by weaving or coiling. Werregue baskets, made by the Waunana people of Columbia, were so tightly coiled and stitched that water could be carried in them. Today, the Waunana use plastic to make their baskets, and the original baskets fetch high prices among collectors.

Modern Baskets

Basket makers like Lois Walpole, who live and work in an urban environment, have developed the art of weaving using modern packaging materials. Cardboard, net, and plastic are woven into colorful, practical baskets using traditional methods. Here are two baskets you can make using modern materials.

Banana-Shaped Basket

This simple basket is made from 6 strips of strong cardboard 1¼ in (3 cm) by 11¾ in (30 cm). Paint the cardboard first using bright paints and let it dry before cutting. Then punch holes in the strips, 1¼ in (3 cm) from each end. Assemble the strips and fasten them at one end with a large paper fastener. Fan out the basket and weave colored twine in and out of the strips before fastening the other end.

strips attached with one fastener

basket shape formed with two fasteners

Loosely weave twine in between the strips before securing the second fastener.

Assemble basket and tighten the twine to keep the shape.

Making a Banana-Shaped Basket

Woven Plate

To make the plate, find some cardboard that is both strong and flexible. Paint it with acrylic colors and cut it into 1¼-in (3 cm) by 11¾-in (30 cm) strips. Weave the strips together, as shown here, holding them in place with clothes pins.

When the weaving is the correct shape and size, trim any extra pieces of cardboard. Staple the woven strips in position. Measure around the edge of the plate, and cut a 3-in (8 cm) cardboard strip to the same length. Fold this in half lengthwise and bind it around the edge, holding it in place with clothes pins. Sew this strip to the plate using colored wire or twine with a blunt-ended needle.

weaving the strips

Making a Woven Plate

adding the binding

Finished Plates and Basket

Woven Boxes

Cardboard Cities

In some parts of the world, there are shanty towns built on the edges of large cities. Here poor people use materials like cardboard, which many would call waste. In other places, the homeless sleep under bridges and in doorways protected by cardboard boxes. The insulating properties of the cardboard help to keep these people warm.

Cardboard Boxes

The production of a cardboard box that could be folded from one piece of flat cardboard revolutionized packaging in the 1850s. Cartons became cheap and easy to produce, but were also disposable. Modern society has become dependent on the cardboard box to package almost everything we buy.

Look at the cartons and boxes used in stores and supermarkets to package food products, toiletries, and many other items. Many have interesting graphics and labeling. A great deal of time and money goes into their design, yet they are rarely reused and most of them are thrown away.

Three-Dimensional Weaving

A cardboard box can be used again as a structure for a three-dimensional weaving. Find a suitable box and seal the top and bottom with tape. Paint all the sides to cover up any printing, and cut a series of notches in the edges. Wind colored plastic twine around these notches. Further twine and tape can then be interwoven, forming a three-dimensional woven cube.

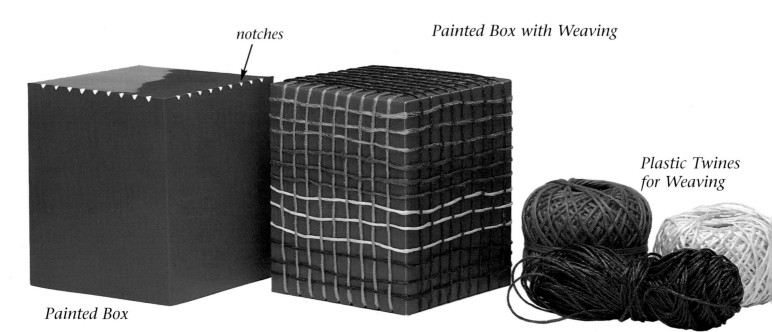

notches

Painted Box with Weaving

Plastic Twines for Weaving

Painted Box

Woven Boxes

These boxes are woven from strips of flexible cardboard. Use any scrap cardboard — cereal boxes are ideal — painting them first to disguise any printed surface.

Cut ten cardboard strips 1¼ in (3 cm) by 17½ in (45 cm), and weave them into place as shown, forming the base of the box. Bend each cardboard strip so it forms a right angle to the base. Cut five strips 1¼ in (3 cm) by 27⅓ in (70 cm) and weave them through these strips, forming the sides of the box. Finish by tucking the ends inside the box.

Finishing the Box

Cut the strip of cardboard 2⅓ in (6 cm) by 25⅓ in (65 cm) and crease it along the center. Fold it over the top edge of the box. Sew the strip into place with colored twine, using a large, blunt-ended needle and blanket stitch. To make a lid, use ten cardboard strips 1¼ in (3 cm) by 9⅓ in (24 cm) and follow the weaving instructions for the box.

Weaving a Box

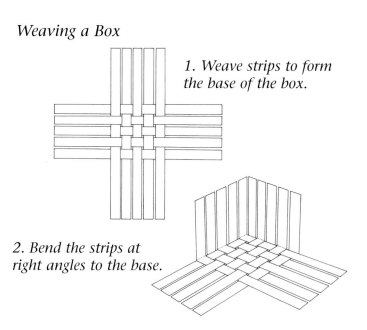

1. Weave strips to form the base of the box.

2. Bend the strips at right angles to the base.

3. Weave strips around the box to form the sides.

Finished Woven Box and Lid

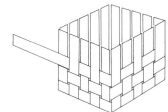

Figures from Foil

Packaging with Foil

Beteween 1910 and 1920, two new materials were introduced to the packaging industry. They were aluminum foil and cellophane. They were used to wrap many different products, especially food, keeping it clean and fresh. Because it is such a practical material, aluminum is used extensively today to package a wide variety of foods, from fresh and frozen items to carbonated drinks.

Aluminum is an attractive material for packaging, because it is lightweight and easy to bend. It is also an easy material to recycle. Seattle has introduced a recycling program that recovers 45 percent of its waste. From 1·7 million tons of aluminum thrown away in a year, 1.7 million tons are recycled. Cans are 20 percent cheaper to make from recycled aluminum, and the process requires only 5 percent of the energy.

Working with Foil

Foil is a soft material, and so it is easy to shape. Collect some discarded foil containers, such as plates or small pie tins; make sure they are cleaned thoroughly before using them. Foil can be cut with scissors, but be careful of any sharp edges.

Making Foil Figures

Find several clean, foil plates of different shapes and sizes. A large, round plate can make the base for a foil figure. Draw patterns on the foil with a ballpoint pen. The pen will leave impressions in the soft foil. Cut out sections and shapes from the smaller plates for features, and staple them to the base. Finally, cut a slot in the base of a small foil dish and use it as a stand for the foil figure.

Foil Figure

back of cardboard

Making a Foil Hanging

To make a foil picture, first cut a base out of thin cardboard, about 12 sq in (30 sq cm). Cut a piece of foil, about 2 in (5 cm) larger than the cardboard. Crinkle the foil and then carefully flatten it. Glue it to the cardboard, overlapping the sides as shown here.

Find a clean foil plate that is about 8 in (20 cm) in diameter. Draw a face design on the plate, using a ballpoint pen to make patterns. Cut out the eyes and mouth with scissors. Glue the face to the foil backing.

Covering Cardboard with Foil

Coloring Foil

To give the background foil a polished, metallic look, try painting it with colored ink. Be careful not to flatten the crinkled texture. Tape two flip-top tabs to the back of the picture, and use them to pin it to the wall.

Making a Foil Face

Second-Chance Art

Found Objects

Artists are often inspired by the shape of a particular object when they create a work of art. Picasso used a toy car to shape the head on his baboon sculpture. He created many sculptures out of found objects and then cast them in bronze. He also made a bull's head out of a bicycle saddle and a pair of handlebars.

Junk Figures

A Second Chance

Unnecessary packaging adds to the mountains of trash accumulating in our throwaway world. Products are packaged in many ways, but paper containers coated with wax or lined with plastic cannot be recycled. It is these items that we need to reuse.

Give all packaging a second chance. Can an empty container or bottle be used again in a practical way, or does it suggest to you a particular figure or shape? You may be able to use it in a fun way. Look at the ideas here, and try to think up some of your own.

Junk Figures

These figures have been made from a range of plastic bottles and containers. Paint the containers first with acrylic paints, and then glue scraps of colored paper, tape, and fabric to them. Half fill them with sand or gravel and use them as bowling pins.

Tubular Figures

Cardboard tubes and rolls are very strong structures that are used to support many household products. Here is a way to put them to good use.

Collect a selection of different sized tubes. Large tubes will be needed for the head and body, with smaller-diameter tubes for the neck, arms, and legs. Paint the tubes or cover them in colored wrapping paper before assembling the figures.

Using a large needle, make holes in the tubes, as shown in the diagram. Then thread stiff wire through the holes to make the joints, securing each end with a loop.

Different Cardboard Tubes

Making Tubular Figures

Thread stiff wire through holes to make joints.

Attach cardboard hands and feet to the figures.

19

Plant Pots

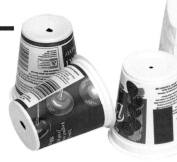

Make drainage holes in plastic containers.

Growing

Plastic containers are ideal to use as plant pots and are now widely used by gardeners as a cheaper alternative to terra-cotta. All the containers you need for growing seeds and root cuttings (part of the part that includes the root) can be recycled from everyday household items.

Choosing Containers

Plastic yogurt cups, ice cream and margarine containers can all be used as plant pots for young seedlings. Larger plastic or foil food trays are ideal for sowing small seeds. However, all these containers must be thoroughly washed before reusing, and for plants to grow, the containers must have adequate drainage holes.

Collect suitable containers and seeds. If you do not have a yard, you can grow seeds successfully on a window ledge. It is also easy to grow house plants from cuttings. Keep a record of their growth in a journal.

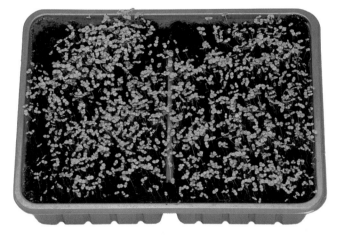

Seedlings and Cuttings Growing in Plastic Containers

Notebook to Record Plant Growth

April 26th
Planted cuttings—
Spider plant, cactus,
& succulents

Seedlings—
Mustard & Cress
½ in (1 cm) tall.

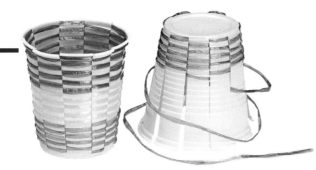

Woven Pots

Decorated Pots

Decorating Pots

Containers can be used just as they are once they have been washed. However, you can make them more decorative. Cut an odd number of slits in the sides and weave lengths of colored tapes in and out, or cover them with colored plastic twine. Attach the twine to the pots with strips of double-sided tape.

Bottle Garden

Bottle Gardens

Plants growing in a bottle create their own ecosystem and once they are watered, they need very little attention. You will need a large, clear, bottle — a disused storage jar is ideal. Put a 1½-in (4 cm) layer of gravel in the bottom of the jar, with a 4-in (10 cm) layer of soil on top. Find out which plants grow well in a damp atmosphere, and plant them in the bottle. When you next use disposable plastic cutlery, take it home and wash it. It makes ideal tools for pot gardening. Use a plastic bottle as a watering can.

Bottle Garden Tools

21

Musical Material

Early Instruments

The first musical instruments were made from natural materials — wood is an ideal material for drums because it makes a good sound when it is hit. Seeds inside gourds make rattles and shakers. People have always used whatever materials were at hand to make music. You can create a whole orchestra of sounds by using packaging and junk materials that might otherwise be thrown away.

Many of the instruments featured on this page have their origins in the distant past. Music has always been a source of pleasure, as well as an important means of communication. Much African music is based on speech. The pitch of African "talking" drums imitates the natural sounds of the language.

Junk Drums and Shakers

Experiment with a selection of plastic, tin, and cardboard containers. Each will give a different sound when it is struck like a drum. If the same containers are filled with dry materials like seeds or sand, you will hear a whole range of new sounds when you shake them. To make a drum, cut the end off a large balloon and stretch it over the open container, taping it firmly in place. Decorate the drums and shakers with colored cardboard, tape, and stickers.

Dried Materials for Shakers

Container Drums

Shakers

Decorate drums and shakers with colored cardboard, tape, and stickers.

Bottle Top Castanets

Rattles, Tambourines, and Castanets

Rattles are the simplest musical instrument and are found worldwide. In Kenya, rattles like the one shown here are made from bottle tops threaded on a wire loop. Castanets and tambourines are favorite instruments to accompany dancers. Metal or plastic lids attached to flexible card make excellent castanets. The tambourine is made from two foil dishes stapled together and decorated with ribbons and bells.

Bottle Top Rattle

Tambourine

Plastic Didgeridoo

The didgeridoo is a traditional Aboriginal instrument. It is used in rituals to communicate with ancestors. This music is a series of almost continuous notes. Aboriginal musicians have developed the special breathing skills needed to make the familiar sounds. This didgeridoo is made from a one-yard (one meter) piece of plastic or cardboard tubing which makes the humming sounds stronger.

Didgeridoo

Decorate with colored tape and stickers.

Shadow Puppets

The first puppets were made in Asia, where they were used to bring to life ancient myths and legends. Cambodia, Thailand, Malaysia, and Bali have long-established shadow puppet traditions. The shadow puppets of Java are perhaps the most splendid. Jointed puppets are operated by a series of long rods, which keep the shadow of the puppetmaster away from the performance.

Making the Theater

1. Cut the theater from a large box.

2. To make the slotted floor, measure and score a piece of cardboard.

3. Carefully fold the cardboard to make a series of parallel slots.

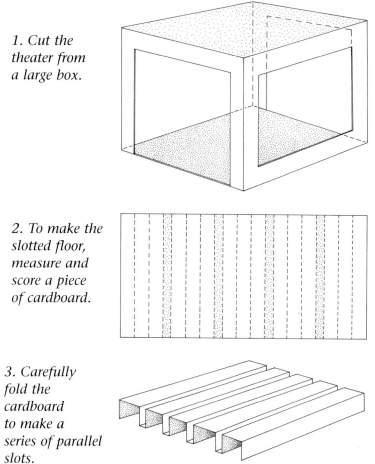

Collecting Materials

It is simple to set up a theater and make puppets. The main material you need is plenty of scrap cardboard of different thicknesses. The theater is made from a large, strong cardboard box, the scenery and puppets are made from thinner cardboard that can be painted.

Planning the Story Line

Before you make the puppets and design the scenery, you will need to decide on a story line for a play. Write an outline, keeping your ideas very simple. Two scenes and four characters will be sufficient. You can only operate two puppets at a time.

Making the Theater

Cut the front and sides out of a large cardboard box, as shown here. The puppets slide along in slots in the stage floor. To make the floor, find a piece of thin cardboard and cut it to the same width as the theater. Score and fold the cardboard as shown, making a series of parallel slots in the cardboard. Make sure the wooden dowels that are attached to the puppets fit into the slots and move freely.

Finally, paint the theater and decorate it with colored paper scraps or wrapping paper.

Puppet Characters

Sketch the puppet shapes on paper before drawing them on cardboard. These puppets are always seen in profile, so make sure that some of your characters are designed to enter from the left and others from the right.

Paint the puppets, cut them out and then glue them to pieces of wooden dowel. Make pieces of scenery from cardboard and position them in the slots.

The Puppet Theater

Glue the puppets to pieces of wooden dowel.

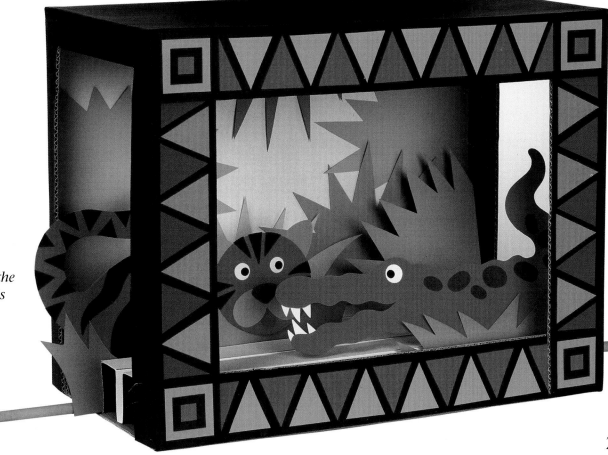

Make sure the wooden rods slide easily in the slots.

Secondhand Toys

Children at Play

Toys made from salvaged found objects and materials are familiar in Africa today. In Botswana, they are now produced for export. Often the name of the original manufacturer is still visible on the finished toy, strangely this adds to the value. There are many African children who make toys from discarded objects, because no other toys are available. In Kenya, footballs are sometimes made out of plastic bags bound into a ball shape with string.

Jointed Toys

Jointed toys became popular in Europe during the eighteenth century. By the nineteenth century, they had become more complicated and were operated in a number of ways. The coiled spring was the most common method used. When the nineteenth century came to an end, the mass-produced, tin-plate toy industry was underway. Moving toys have been popular with children ever since. The majority of today's toys are made from plastic and are battery powered.

Robot

This simple moving toy is made up of various shapes cut from plastic scraps. A snap attached to each joint allows it to move freely. Use plastic that is stiff, yet thin enough for holes to be punched through to make the joints.

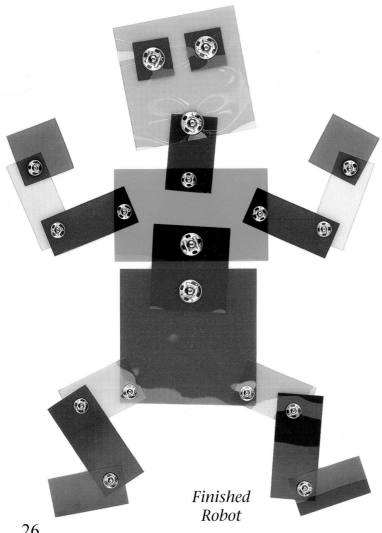

Finished Robot

Punch holes in plastic pieces.

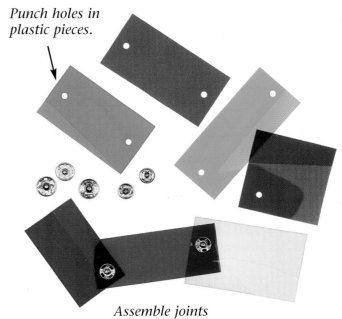

Assemble joints with large snaps.

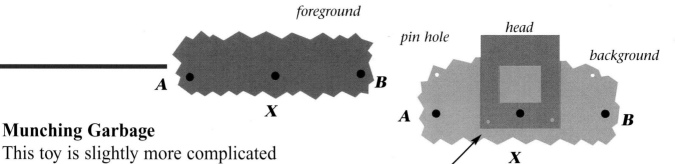
foreground

pin hole *head* *background*

A   X   B

A   X   B

string hole

Munching Garbage

This toy is slightly more complicated and moves on a pivot, called the *fulcrum*. Cut the main pieces from strong, scrap cardboard. Paint or cover them with a collage of paper, foil, and plastic scraps. Make holes in the pieces, as shown.

Fix a weight to the head with two pieces of string. Attach the head to the background at point X using a split pin, making sure it moves freely. Assemble the foreground and background pieces at points A and B, using paper fasteners. Pin the "garbage dump" to a wall, swing the weight, and see the robot munch away.

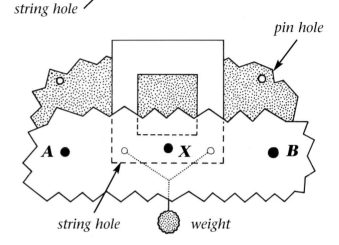
pin hole

A   X   B

string hole   *weight*

Assembling the Garbage Dump Monster

Garbage Dump Monster

swinging weight

27

Moving Wheels

Moving Around

You can create movement by building a system of connected cogs and wheels out of salvaged (found) materials. Movement goes from one part of the machine to the next. A small cog connected with a large cog turns more frequently. These wheels do not move forward, they simply turn around and around. Cog wheels can be seen inside old, mechanical clocks and watches.

Cogs and Wheels from Junk

Collect a variety of circular junk items, such as shallow cheese containers and lids of different sizes. Glue pieces of lollipop sticks to each cog as shown here. Make a hole through the middle of each cog, then attach them to a cardboard base. Make sure the cogs rotate freely and the spokes connect. When one cog is turned, all the others should move, too.

Making the cogs.

Moving Cogs and Wheels

Glue sticks firmly to lid.

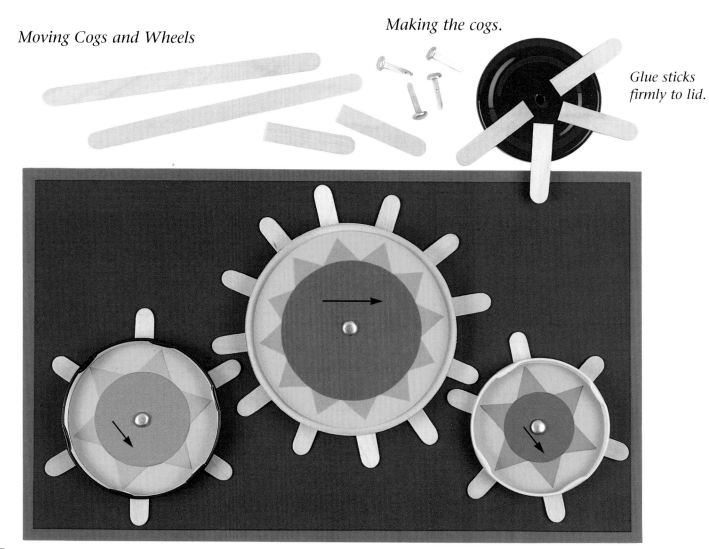

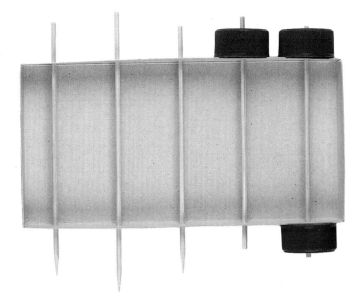

Moving Wheels

Here is an idea for making a three-dimensional machine that will move along a surface when it is pushed or pulled. This time you will need to collect an even number of small plastic lids that are all the same size.

Making a Rolling Bug

Find or make a long, narrow box about 8 in (20 cm) by 4 in (10 cm) by 1¼ in (3 cm) in size. Make a series of small holes along each side of the box — one hole for each pair of wheels. Use wooden barbecue sticks for axles, and thread them through the holes.

Assembling the Wheels and Axles

Make a hole in the middle of each lid. Push them onto the axle, cutting off any extra length. Attach each lid to its axle with a blob of glue. Attach a piece of string to the front of the box to pull it. Make sure it moves smoothly on the wheels.

Decorate the box with scraps of plastic, colored paper, and yarn, and turn it into a rolling bug.

Rolling Bug

Glossary

Aborigines An ancient people who lived in Australia long before it was discovered by Europeans.

axle A bar or shaft connecting the wheels on a vehicle.

biodegradable A material that decomposes naturally.

cuttings Small sections cut from plant stems that form their own roots in water or soil.

dowel A small piece of wood used to join two other pieces of wood together.

ecosystem The interaction between living things within their environment.

fulcrum The pivot around which a lever turns.

gourds Fruit of plants of the cucumber family. In Africa, dried shells were often used to make musical instruments and other artifacts.

graphics The art of drawing to mathematical principles.

gravel A mixture of rock fragments and pebbles.

humid A moist, damp atmosphere.

journal A written daily record in book form.

junk Discarded objects.

labeling Attaching paper, cardboard, or another material to an object to identify it.

landfill sites Large pits that are filled with alternate layers of garbage and earth.

methane gas A colorless, odorless, and flammable gas that can be used as a fuel.

monoprint A repeating pattern created with a unique printing block.

packaging Wrappings and boxes made specially to hold and protect retail items.

Picasso, Pablo Ruiz (1881–1973) A Spanish artist who is looked on by many people as the most inventive and innovative artist of the twentieth century.

portfolio A flat case used to store and carry papers.

rattans The stems of a climbing palm used for wickerwork and canes.

seedlings Young plants grown from seed.

shanty town Part of a town or city where very poor people live in ramshackle huts, often built from discarded materials.

For More Information

Books to Read

Kids Weaving: Projects for Kids of all Ages, Sarah Swett (Stewart, Tabori and Chang, 2005)

My DIY (The Stylin' Girl's Guide to DIY Projects), Kimberley Potts (Adams Media Corporation, 2005)

Nature's Art Box, Laura C. Martin (Storey Publishing, 2003)

Puppet Mania!, John E. Kennedy (North Light Books, 2004)

Puppets (Crafts from Many Cultures), Meryl Doney (Gareth Stevens Publishing, 2004)

Recycled Crafts Box, Laura C. Martin (Storey Publishing, 2004)

The Kids Multi-Cultural Craft Book, Roberta Gould (Williamson Publishing Company, 2003)

The Super Duper Art and Craft Activity Book, Lynn Gordon (Chronicle Books, 2005)

Places to Visit

American Visionary Art Museum,
800 Key Highway, Baltimore, Maryland 21230
(Displaying art from recycled materials including customized Art Cars', sculpture, and mosaics)

Boston Children's Museum,
300 Congress Street, Boston MA 02210
(Includes The Recycle Shop, a children's activity center where re-used materials can be transformed into art projects, and weaving exhibits, including large-scale looms for children to use.)

Metropolitan Museum of Art,
1000 Fifth Avenue, New York, New York 10028
(Wide range of exhibits, including jewelry, mosaics, sculpture, block printing, and textiles and dyeing)

The Museum of Printing History,
1324 West Clay Street, Houston, Texas 77019
(Runs workshops for children on papermaking and printmaking)

UCM Museum,
22275 Hwy 36, Abita Springs, LA 70420, Ph: 985-892-2624
(Small, unusual collection of art made from recycled materials, mosaics, and more)

Web Sites

Due to the changing nature of Internet links, PowerKids Press has developed an online list of Web sites related to the subject of this book. This site is regularly updated. Please use this link to access this list:
www.powerkidslinks.com/everydayart/packaging

Index